Referees' C and Players to the Laws Association Football

1992–1993

Authorized by the International
Football Association Board

Revised edition, August 1992

PAN BOOKS

LONDON, SYDNEY AND AUCKLAND

This edition published 1992 by
Pan Books Ltd, Cavaye Place, London SW10 9PG

© 1992 by The Football Association
16 Lancaster Gate, London W2

ISBN 0 330 31927 2

Amendments to Laws and Decisions made
in 1992 are indicated in italics

Phototypeset by Intype, London
Printed in England by Clays Ltd, St Ives plc

THE FOOTBALL TRUST was founded by the Pool Promoters Association in 1979 and, with money made available from 'Spotting-the-Ball', it was empowered to provide funds for the benefit of football in general, with particular emphasis on tackling any associated social problems.

Over the years the Trust has assisted with the improvement of safety at League club grounds, with Football and the Community schemes, with the provision of improved pitches and hard surface play areas, and with specific security measures such as the installation of closed circuit television at League grounds.

Contents

THE LAWS OF THE GAME

Notes

Subject to the agreement of the National Association concerned and provided the principles of these Laws are maintained, the Laws may be modified in their application for matches for players of under 16 years of age, for women's football and for veterans' football (over 35 years).

Any or all of the following modifications are permissible:—
  (a) size of the field of play;
  (b) size, weight and material of ball;
  (c) width between the goal-posts and height of the cross-bar from the ground;
  (d) the duration of the periods of play;
  (e) number of substitutions.

Further modifications are only possible with the consent of the International Football Association Board.

The Field of Play and appurtenances shall be as shown in the plan below.

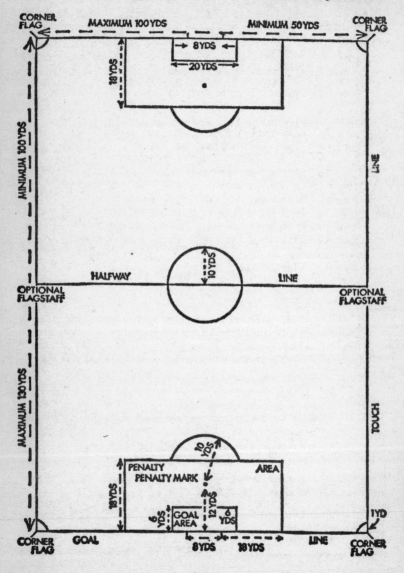

Law One

(1) **Dimensions.** The field of play shall be rectangular, its length being not more than 130 yards nor less than 100 yards and its breadth not more than 100 yards nor less than 50 yards. (In International Matches the length shall be not more than 120 yards nor less than 110 yards and the breadth not more than 80 yards nor less than 70 yards.) The length shall in all cases exceed the breadth.

(2) **Marking.** The field of play shall be marked with distinctive lines, not more than 5 inches in width, not by a V-shaped rut, in accordance with the plan, the longer boundary lines being called the touch lines and the shorter the goal-lines. A flag on a post not less than 5 feet high and having a non-pointed top, shall be placed at each corner; a similar flag-post may be placed opposite the halfway-line on each side of the field of play, not less than 1 yard outside the touch-line. A halfway-line shall be marked out across the field of play. The centre of the field of play shall be indicated by a suitable mark and a circle with a 10 yards radius shall be marked round it.

(3) **The Goal-Area.** At each end of the field of play two lines shall be drawn at right-angles to the goal-line, 6 yards from each goal-post. These shall extend into the field of play for a distance of 6 yards and shall be joined by a line drawn parallel with the goal-line. Each of the spaces enclosed by these lines and the goal-line shall be called the goal-area.

(4) **The Penalty-Area.** At each end of the field of play two lines shall be drawn at right-angles to the goal-line, 18 yards from each goal-post. These shall extend into the field of play for a distance of 18 yards and shall be joined by a line drawn parallel with the goal-line. Each of the spaces enclosed by these lines and the goal-line shall be called a penalty-area. A suitable mark shall be made within each penalty-area, 12 yards from the mid-point of the goal-line, measured along an undrawn line at right angles thereto. These shall be the penalty-kick marks. From each penalty-kick mark an arc of a circle, having a radius of 10 yards, shall be drawn outside the penalty-area.

(5) **The Corner-Area.** From each corner flag-post a quarter circle, having a radius of 1 yard, shall be drawn inside the field of play.

(6) **The Goals.** The goals shall be placed on the centre of each goal-line

and shall consist of two upright posts, equidistant from the corner-flags and 8 yards apart (inside measurement), joined by a horizontal cross-bar the lower edge of which shall be 8 ft. from the ground. The width and depth of the goal-posts and the width and depth of the cross-bars shall not exceed 5 inches (12 cm) The goal-posts and the cross-bars shall have the same width.

Nets may be attached to the posts, cross-bars and ground behind the goals. They should be appropriately supported and be so placed as to allow the goalkeeper ample room.

INTERNATIONAL BOARD DECISIONS

1. In International Matches the dimensions of the field of play shall be: maximum 110 metres × 75 metres; minimum 100 metres × 64 metres.

2. National Associations must adhere strictly to these dimensions. Each National Association organizing an International Match must advise the Visiting Association, before the match, of the place and the dimensions of the field of play.

3. The Board has approved this table of measurements for the Laws of the Game.

	Metres			*Metres*
130 yards ..	.. 120	1 yard ..	.. 1
120 yards ..	.. 110	8 feet ..	.. 2.44
110 yards ..	.. 100	5 feet ..	.. 1.50
100 yards ..	.. 90	28 inches ..	.. 0.71
80 yards ..	.. 75	27 inches ..	.. 0.68
70 yards ..	.. 64	9 inches ..	.. 0.22
50 yards ..	.. 45	5 inches ..	.. 0.12
18 yards ..	.. 16.50	½ inch ..	.. 12.7 mm
12 yards ..	.. 11	⅜ inch ..	.. 10 mm
10 yards ..	.. 9.15	14 ozs. = 396 grams	
8 yards ..	.. 7.32	16 ozs. = 453 grams	
6 yards ..	.. 5.50	8.5 lb./sq.in. = 600 gr/cm^2	
		15.6 lb./sq. in. = 1,100 gr/cm^2	

4. The goal-line shall be marked the same width as the depth of the goal-posts and the cross-bar so that the goal-line and goal-posts will conform in the same interior and exterior edges.

5. The 6 yards (for the outline of the goal-area) and the 18 yards (for the

outline of the penalty-area) which have to be measured along the goal-line, must start from the inner sides of the goalposts.

6. The space within the inside areas of the field of play includes the width of the lines marking these areas.

7. All Associations shall provide standard equipment, particularly in International Matches, when the Laws of the Game must be complied with in every respect and especially with regard to the size of the ball and other equipment which must conform to the regulations. All cases of failure to provide standard equipment must be reported to FIFA.

8. In a match played under the rules of a competition if the cross-bar becomes displaced or broken play shall be stopped and the match abandoned unless the cross-bar has been repaired and replaced in position or a new one provided without such being a danger to the players. A rope is not considered to be a satisfactory substitute for a cross-bar.

In a friendly match, by mutual consent, play may be resumed without the cross-bar provided it has been removed and no longer constitutes a danger to the players. In these circumstances, a rope may be used as a substitute for a cross-bar. If a rope is not used and the ball crosses the goal-line at a point which in the opinion of the Referee is below where the cross-bar should have been he shall award a goal.

The game shall be restarted by the Referee dropping the ball at the place where it was when play was stopped, unless it was within the goal area at that time, in which case it shall be dropped on that part of the goal area line which runs parallel to the goal-line, at the point nearest to where the ball was when play was stopped.

9. National Associations may specify such maximum and minimum dimensions for the cross-bars and goal-posts, within the limits laid down in Law 1, as they consider appropriate.

10. Goal-posts and cross-bars must be made of wood, metal or other approved material as decided from time to time by the International FA Board. They may be square, rectangular, round, half round, or elliptical in shape. Goal-posts and cross-bars made of other materials and in other shapes are not permitted. The goal-posts must be of white colour.

11. 'Curtain-raisers' to International Matches should only be played following agreement on the day of the match, and taking into account the condition of the field of play, between representatives of the two Associations and the Referee (of the International Match).

12. National Associations, particularly in International Matches, should

restrict the number of photographers around the field of play, have a line ('photographers' line') marked behind the goal-lines at least two metres from the corner-flag going through a point situated at least 3.5 metres behind the intersection of the goal-line with the line marking the goal area to a point situated at least six metres behind the goal-posts, prohibit photographers from passing over these lines and forbid the use of artificial lighting in the form of 'flash-lights'.

Advice to Referees

Visit the ground in good time before a match to see that everything is in order. If through bad weather or negligence the state of the ground is such that it may endanger the players, refuse to sanction play. If the lines are not properly marked see that, if time allows, it is done before the match.

Examine the goal-nets before every match, ensure that they are properly pegged down and that they are intact.

Law Two

THE BALL

The ball shall be spherical; the outer casing shall be of leather or other approved materials. No material shall be used in its construction which might prove dangerous to the players.

The circumference of the ball shall not be more than 28 inches and not less than 27 inches. The weight of the ball at the start of the game shall not be more than 16 oz nor less than 14 oz. The pressure shall be equal to 0.6–1.1 atmosphere (= 600–1,100 gr/cm²) at sea level. The ball shall not be changed during the game unless authorized by the Referee.

INTERNATIONAL BOARD DECISIONS

1. The ball used in any match shall be considered the property of the Association or Club on whose ground the match is played, and at the close of play it must be returned to the Referee.

2. The International Board, from time to time, shall decide what constitutes approved materials. Any approved material shall be certified as such by the International Board.

3. The Board has approved these equivalents of the weights specified in the law:

$$14 \text{ to } 16 \text{ ounces} = 396 \text{ to } 453 \text{ grammes.}$$

4. If the ball bursts or becomes deflated during the course of a match, the game shall be stopped and restarted by dropping the new ball at the place where the first ball became defective, unless it was within the goal area at that time, in which case it shall be dropped on that part of the goal area line which runs parallel to the goal-line, at the point nearest to where the ball was when play was stopped.

5. If this happens during a stoppage of the game (place-kick, goal-kick, corner-kick, free-kick, penalty-kick or throw-in) the game shall be restarted accordingly.

Law Three

NUMBER OF PLAYERS

(1) A match shall be played by two teams, each consisting of not more than eleven players, one of whom shall be the goalkeeper.

(2) Substitutes may be used in any match played under the rules of an official competition under the jurisdiction of FIFA, Confederations or National Associations, subject to the following conditions:–

- (a) that the authority of the International Association(s) or National Association(s) concerned, has been obtained;
- (b) that, subject to the restriction contained in the following paragraph (c) the rules of a competition shall state how many, if any, substitutes may be nominated and how many of those nominated may be used;
- (c) that a team shall not be permitted to use more than two substitutes in any match, who must be chosen from not more than five players whose names may (subject to the rules of the competition) be required to be given to the Referee prior to the commencement of the match.

(3) Substitutes may be used in any other match, provided that the two teams concerned reach agreement on a maximum number, not exceeding five, and that the terms of such agreement are intimated to the Referee, before the match. If the Referee is not informed, or if the teams fail to

reach agreement, no more than 2 substitutes shall be permitted. In all cases the substitutes must be chosen from not more than five players whose names may be required to be given to the Referee prior to the commencement of the match.

(4) Any of the other players may change places with the goalkeeper, provided that the Referee is informed before the change is made, and provided also, that the change is made during a stoppage in the game.

(5) When a goalkeeper or any other player is to be replaced by a substitute, the following conditions shall be observed:—

- (a) the Referee shall be informed of the proposed substitution, before it is made;
- (b) the substitute shall not enter the field of play until the player he is replacing has left, and then only after having received a signal from the Referee;
- (c) he shall enter the field during a stoppage in the game, and at the halfway-line;
- (d) a player who has been replaced shall not take any further part in the game;
- (e) a substitute shall be subject to the authority and jurisdiction of the Referee whether called upon to play or not.
- (f) the substitution is completed when the substitute enters the field of play, from which moment he becomes a player and the player whom he is replacing ceases to be a player.

Punishment

- (a) Play shall not be stopped for an infringement of paragraph 4. The players concerned shall be cautioned immediately the ball goes out of play.
- (b) If a substitute enters the field of play without the authority of the Referee, play shall be stopped. The substitute shall be cautioned and removed from the field or sent off according to the circumstances. The game shall be restarted by the Referee dropping the ball at the place where it was when play was stopped, unless it was within the goal area at that time, in which case it shall be dropped on that part of the goal area line which runs parallel to the goal-line, at the point nearest to where the ball was when play was stopped.
- (c) For any other infringement of this Law, the player concerned shall be cautioned, and if the game is stopped by the Referee to

administer the caution, it shall be restarted by an indirect free-kick, to be taken by a player of the opposing team, from the place where the ball was when play was stopped, subject to the over-riding conditions imposed in Law 13.

(d) If a Competition's rules require the names of substitutes to be given to the Referee, prior to the commencement of the match, then failure to do so will mean that no substitutes can be permitted.

INTERNATIONAL BOARD DECISIONS

1. The minimum number of players in a team is left to the discretion of National Associations.

2. The Board is of the opinion that a match should not be considered valid if there are fewer than seven players in either of the teams.

3. A player who has been ordered off before play begins may only be replaced by one of the named substitutes. The kick-off must not be delayed to allow the substitute to join his team.

A player who has been ordered off after play has started may not be replaced. A named substitute who has been ordered off, either before or after play has started, may not be replaced. (This decision only relates to players who are ordered off under Law 12. It does not apply to players who have infringed Law 4.)

Advice to Referees

Note which players are acting as goalkeepers at the start of the game; until informed of a change, allow no other player to take up or claim the privileges attached to the position.

Do not referee unsanctioned matches or competitions.

Law Four

PLAYERS' EQUIPMENT

(1) (a) The basic compulsory equipment of a player shall consist of a jersey or shirt, shorts, stockings, shinguards and footwear.

(b) A player shall not wear anything which is dangerous to another player.

(2) Shinguards, which must be covered entirely by the stockings, shall be made of a suitable material (rubber, plastic, polyurethane or similar substance) and shall afford a reasonable degree of protection.

(3) The goalkeeper shall wear colours which distinguish him from the other players and from the referee.

Punishment

For any infringement of this Law, the player at fault shall be instructed to leave the field of play by the referee, to adjust his equipment or obtain any missing equipment, when the ball next ceases to be in play, unless by then the player has already corrected his equipment. Play shall not be stopped immediately for an infringement of this Law. A player who is instructed to leave the field to adjust his equipment or obtain missing equipment shall not return without first reporting to the referee, who shall satisfy himself that the player's equipment is in order. The player shall only re-enter the game at a moment when the ball has ceased to be in play.

INTERNATIONAL BOARD DECISIONS

1. In International Matches, International Competitions, International Club Competitions and friendly matches between clubs of different National Associations, the Referee, prior to the start of the game, shall inspect the players' equipment, and prevent any player whose equipment does not conform to the requirements of this Law from playing until such time as it does comply.

The rules of any competition may include a similar provision.

2. If the Referee finds that a player is wearing articles not permitted by the Laws and which may constitute a danger to other players, he shall order him to take them off. If he fails to carry out the Referee's instruction, the player shall not take part in the match.

3. A player who has been prevented from taking part in the game or a player who has been sent off the field for infringing Law 4 **must** report to the Referee during a stoppage of the game and may not enter or re-enter the field of play unless and until the Referee has satisfied himself that the player is no longer infringing Law 4.

4. A player who has been prevented from taking part in a game or who has been sent off because of an infringement of Law 4, and who enters

or re-enters the field of play to join or rejoin his team in breach of the conditions of Law 12(*j*), shall be cautioned.

If the Referee stops the game to administer the caution, the game shall be restarted by an indirect free-kick, taken by a player of the opposing side, from the place where the ball was when the Referee stopped the game, subject to the over-riding conditions imposed in Law 13.

Advice to Referees

If asked to do so, examine the players' boots or other equipment before the match or during the interval. If you have any reason for doubt you may require to examine a player's boots, etc at any time.

For infringement of this Law there is no need to wait for any appeal; having noted the offence, enforce the punishment immediately. The offence need not be reported.

Law Five

REFEREES

A Referee shall be appointed to officiate in each game. His authority and the exercise of the powers granted to him by the Laws of the Game commence as soon as he enters the field of play.

His power of penalizing shall extend to offences committed when play has been temporarily suspended, or when the ball is out of play. His decision on points of fact connected with the play shall be final, so far as the result of the game is concerned.

He shall:–

(*a*) Enforce the Laws.
(*b*) Refrain from penalizing in cases where he is satisfied that, by doing so, he would be giving an advantage to the offending team.
(*c*) Keep a record of the game; act as timekeeper and allow the full or agreed time, adding thereto all time lost through accident or other cause.
(*d*) Have discretionary power to stop the game for any infringement of the Laws and to suspend or terminate the game whenever, by reasons of the elements, interference by spectators, or other cause, he deems such stoppage necessary. In such a case he shall submit a detailed report to the competent authority, within the stipulated

time, and in accordance with the provisions set up by the National Association under whose jurisdiction the match was played. Reports will be deemed to be made when received in the ordinary course of post.

(e) *From the time he enters the field of play, caution and show a yellow card to any player guilty of misconduct or ungentlemanly behaviour. In such cases the referee shall send the name of the offender to the competent authority, within the stipulated time,* and in accordance with the provisions set up by the National Association under whose jurisdiction the match was played. Reports will be deemed to be made when received in the ordinary course of post.*

(f) Allow no person other than the players and Linesmen to enter the field of play without his permission

(g) Stop the game if, in his opinion, a player has been seriously injured; have the player removed as soon as possible from the field of play, and immediately resume the game. If a player is slightly injured, the game shall not be stopped until the ball has ceased to be in play. A player who is able to go to the touch- or goal-line for attention of any kind, shall not be treated on the field of play.

(h) *Send off the field of play and show a red card to any player who, in his opinion, is guilty of violent conduct, serious foul play, the use of foul or abusive language or who persists in misconduct after having received a caution.*

(i) Signal for recommencement of the game after all stoppages.

(j) Decide that the ball provided for a match meets with the requirements of Law 2.

INTERNATIONAL BOARD DECISIONS

1. Referees in International Matches shall wear a blazer or blouse the colour of which is distinctive from the colours worn by the contesting teams.

2. Referees for International Matches will be selected from a neutral country unless the countries concerned agree to appoint their own officials.

3. The Referee must be chosen from the official list of International Referees. This need not apply to Amateur and Youth International matches.

4. The Referee shall report to the appropriate authority misconduct or

* In England, within two days. Sunday not included.

any misdemeanour on the part of spectators, officials, players, named substitutes or other persons which take place either on the field of play or in its vicinity at any time prior to, during, or after the match in question so that appropriate action can be taken by the authority concerned.

5. Linesmen are assistants of the Referee. In no case shall the Referee consider the intervention of a Linesman if he himself has seen the incident and from his position on the field, is better able to judge. With this reserve, and the Linesman neutral, the Referee can consider the intervention and if the information of the Linesman applies to that phase of the game immediately before the scoring of a goal, the Referee may act thereon and cancel the goal.

6. The Referee, however, can only reverse his first decision so long as the game has not been restarted.

7. If the Referee has decided to apply the advantage clause and to let the game proceed, he cannot revoke his decision if the presumed advantage has not been realized, even though he has not, by any gesture, indicated his decision. This does not exempt the offending player from being dealt with by the Referee.

8. The Laws of the Game are intended to provide that games should be played with as little interference as possible, and in this view it is the duty of Referees to penalize only deliberate breaches of the Law. Constant whistling for trifling and doubtful breaches produces bad feeling and loss of temper on the part of the players and spoils the pleasure of spectators.

9. By para. (d) of Law 5 the Referee is empowered to terminate a match in the event of grave disorder, but he has no power or right to decide, in such event, that either team is disqualified and thereby the loser of the match. He must send a detailed report to the proper authority who alone has power to deal further with this matter.

10. If a player commits two infringements of a different nature at the same time, the Referee shall punish the more serious offence.

11. It is the duty of the Referee to act upon the information of neutral Linesmen with regard to incidents that do not come under the personal notice of the Referee.

12. The Referee shall not allow any person to enter the field until play has stopped, and only then, if he has given him a signal to do so, nor shall he allow coaching from the boundary lines.

Advice to Referees

To referee in such a way that you will win the respect of players and spectators:—

   (a) Learn to understand every Law.
   (b) Be absolutely fair and impartial in every decision.
   (c) Keep physically fit and in good training.

Only suspend or terminate a match on account of the weather after very careful consideration.

When cautioning a player, state he is being cautioned and inquire his name, and that if he persists in misconduct after having received a caution he will be ordered off the field. *The Referee will only show the yellow card after this procedure has been completed.*

Note the procedure if a player is cautioned; a Referee who fails to report misconduct which came under his notice may be suspended, if it is proved to the satisfaction of the Council that the case of misconduct should have been further investigated.

If a player is sent off for a second cautionable offence in a match, the Referee is required to show both the yellow and the red card simultaneously in one hand. For a single offence requiring an immediate expulsion, only the red card is shown after the standard procedure.

Compare watches with the Linesmen, both before the game and at half-time.

Do not trust to memory alone in keeping a record of the game; note on paper the time of start and the time at which, if no extra time has to be allowed, half-time and the end of the game will fall due.

Note also the goals as they are scored.

The application of the provisions of (g) should be strictly observed.

Law Six

LINESMEN

Two Linesmen shall be appointed, whose duty (subject to the decision of the Referee) shall be to indicate:

   (a) When the ball is out of play,
   (b) Which side is entitled to a corner-kick, goal-kick or throw-in,
   (c) When a substitution is desired.

They shall also assist the Referee to control the game in accordance with the Laws. In the event of undue interference or improper conduct by a Linesman, the Referee shall dispense with his services and arrange for a substitute to be appointed. (The matter shall be reported by the Referee to the competent authority.) The Linesmen should be equipped with flags by the Club on whose ground the match is played.

INTERNATIONAL BOARD DECISIONS

1. Linesmen where neutral shall draw the Referee's attention to any breach of the Laws of the Game of which they become aware if they consider that the Referee may not have seen it, but the Referee shall always be the judge of the decision to be taken.

2. National Associations are advised to appoint official Referees of neutral nationality to act as Linesmen in International Matches.

3. In International Matches, Linesmen's flags shall be of a vivid colour – bright reds and yellows. Such flags are recommended for use in all other matches.

4. A Linesman may be subject to disciplinary action only upon a report of the Referee for unjustified interference or insufficient assistance.

Law Seven

DURATION OF THE GAME

The duration of the game shall be two equal periods of 45 minutes, unless otherwise mutually agreed upon, subject to the following:–

- (a) Allowance shall be made in either period for all time lost through substitution, the transport from the field of injured players, time-wasting or other cause, the amount of which shall be a matter for the discretion of the Referee.
- (b) Time shall be extended to permit of a penalty-kick being taken at or after the expiration of the normal period in either half.

At half-time the interval shall not exceed five minutes except by consent of the Referee.

1. If a match has been stopped by the Referee, before the completion of the time specified in the rules, for any reason stated in Law 5 it must be replayed in full unless the rules of the competition concerned provide for the result of the match at the time of such stoppage to stand.

2. Players have a right to an interval at half-time.

Advice to Referees

A Referee has no power to set aside the Rules of Cup and other Competitions where the time to be played is specified.

Normal period means 90 minutes, or if a shorter period is mutually agreed upon and is permissible under the Rules of the Competition the period should be divided in equal halves.

Law Eight

THE START OF PLAY

(a) **At the beginning of the game,** choice of ends and the kick-off shall be decided by the toss of a coin. The team winning the toss shall have the option of choice of ends or the kick-off.

The Referee having given a signal, the game shall be started by a player taking a place-kick (i.e., a kick at the ball while it is stationary on the ground in the centre of the field of play) into his opponents' half of the field of play. Every player shall be in his own half of the field and every player of the team opposing that of the kicker shall remain not less than 10 yards from the ball until it is kicked-off; it shall not be deemed in play until it has travelled the distance of its own circumference. The kicker shall not play the ball a second time until it has been touched or played by another player.

(b) **After a goal has been scored,** the game shall be restarted in like manner by a player of the team losing the goal.

(c) **After half-time;** when restarting after half-time, ends shall be changed and the kick-off shall be taken by a player of the opposite team to that of the player who started the game.

Punishment

For any infringement of this Law, the kick-off shall be retaken, except in the case of the kicker playing the ball again before it has been touched or played by another player; for this offence, an indirect free-kick shall be taken by a player of the opposing team from the place where the infringement occurred, subject to the over-riding conditions imposed in Law 13.

A goal shall not be scored direct from a kick-off.

(d) **After any other temporary suspension;** when restarting the game after a temporary suspension of play from any cause not mentioned elsewhere in these Laws, provided that immediately prior to the suspension the ball has not passed over the touch- or goal-lines, the Referee shall drop the ball at the place where it was when play was suspended, unless it was within the goal area at that time, in which case it shall be dropped on that part of the goal area line which runs parallel to the goal-line, at the point nearest to where the ball was when play was stopped. It shall be deemed in play when it has touched the ground; if, however, it goes over the touch- or goal-lines after it has been dropped by the Referee, but before it is touched by a player, the Referee shall again drop it. A player shall not play the ball until it has touched the ground. If this section of the Law is not complied with the Referee shall again drop the ball.

INTERNATIONAL BOARD DECISIONS

1. If, when the Referee drops the ball, a player infringes any of the Laws before the ball has touched the ground, the player concerned shall be cautioned or sent off the field according to the seriousness of the offence, but a free-kick cannot be awarded to the opposing team because the ball was not in play at the time of the offence. The ball shall therefore be again dropped by the Referee.

2. Kicking-off by persons other than the players competing in a match is prohibited.

Advice to Referees

Note which side kicked-off; the kick must be taken by a player competing in the match. Limit the half-time interval to 5 minutes unless in very exceptional circumstances.

When extra time is necessary, play shall be restarted according to '(a)'. The interval between the end of the normal period of play and the start of the extra period shall be under the jurisdiction of the Referee.

Law Nine

The ball is out of play:–

- (*a*) When it has wholly crossed the goal-line or touch-line, whether on the ground or in the air.
- (*b*) When the game has been stopped by the Referee.

The ball is in play at all other times from the start of the match to the finish including:–

- (*a*) If it rebounds from a goal-post, cross-bar or corner-flag post into the field of play.
- (*b*) If it rebounds off either the Referee or Linesmen when they are in the field of play.
- (*c*) In the event of a supposed infringement of the Laws, until a decision is given.

INTERNATIONAL BOARD DECISIONS

1. The lines belong to the areas of which they are the boundaries. In consequence, the touch-lines and the goal-lines belong to the field of play.

Advice to Referees

To prevent being touched by the ball or interfering with play, Linesmen should, as far as possible, keep out of the field of play.

Law Ten

METHOD OF SCORING

Except as otherwise provided by these Laws, a goal is scored when the whole of the ball has passed over the goal-line, between the goal-posts and under the cross-bar, provided it has not been thrown, carried or intentionally propelled by hand or arm, by a player of the attacking side, except in the case of a goalkeeper, who is within his own penalty area.

The team scoring the greater number of goals during a game shall be the winner; if no goals, or an equal number of goals are scored, the game shall be termed a 'draw'.

1. Law 10 defines the only method according to which a match is won or drawn; no variation whatsoever can be authorized.

2. A goal cannot in any case be allowed if the ball has been prevented by some outside agent from passing over the goal-line. If this happens in the normal course of play, other than at the taking of a penalty-kick, the game must be stopped and restarted by the Referee dropping the ball at the place where the ball came into contact with the interference, unless it was within the goal area at that time, in which case it shall be dropped on that part of the goal area line which runs parallel to the goal-line, at the point nearest to where the ball was when play was stopped.

3. If, when the ball is going into goal, a spectator enters the field before it passes wholly over the goal-line, and tries to prevent a score, a goal shall be allowed if the ball goes into goal, unless the spectator has made contact with the ball or has interfered with play, in which case the Referee shall stop the game and restart it by dropping the ball at the place where the contact or interference occurred, unless it was within the goal area at that time, in which case it shall be dropped on that part of the goal area line which runs parallel to the goal-line, at the point nearest to where the ball was when play was stopped.

Law Eleven

OFF-SIDE

(1) A player is in an off-side position if he is nearer to his opponents' goal-line than the ball, unless:

- (a) he is in his own half of the field of play, or
- (b) he is not nearer to his opponents' goal-line than at least two of his opponents.

(2) A player shall only be declared off-side and penalized for being in an off-side position, if, at the moment the ball touches, or is played by, one of his team, he is, in the opinion of the Referee

    (a) interfering with play or with an opponent, or
    (b) seeking to gain an advantage by being in that position.

(3) A player shall not be declared off-side by the Referee

    (a) merely because of his being in an off-side position, or
    (b) if he receives the ball, direct from a goal-kick, a corner-kick, or a throw-in.

(4) If a player is declared off-side, the Referee shall award an indirect free-kick, which shall be taken by a player of the opposing team from the place where the infringement occurred, unless the offence is committed by a player in his opponents' goal-area, in which case, the free-kick shall be taken from a point anywhere within that half of the goal-area in which the offence occurred.

INTERNATIONAL BOARD DECISIONS

1. Off-side shall not be judged at the moment the player in question receives the ball, but at the moment when the ball is passed to him by one of his own side. A player who is not in an off-side position when one of his colleagues passes the ball to him or takes a free-kick, does not therefore become off-side if he goes forward during the flight of the ball.

2. A player who is level with the second last opponent or with the last two opponents is not in an off-side position.

Law Twelve

FOULS AND MISCONDUCT

A player who intentionally commits any of the following nine offences:—

    (a) Kicks or attempts to kick an opponent;
    (b) Trips an opponent, i.e., throwing or attempting to throw him by the use of the legs or by stooping in front of or behind him;
    (c) Jumps at an opponent;
    (d) Charges an opponent in a violent or dangerous manner;
    (e) Charges an opponent from behind unless the latter be obstructing;
    (f) Strikes or attempts to strike an opponent or spits at him;
    (g) Holds an oppponent;
    (h) Pushes an opponent;

(*i*) Handles the ball, i.e., carries, strikes or propels the ball with his hand or arm. (This does not apply to the goalkeeper within his own penalty-area);

shall be penalized by the award of a **direct free-kick** to be taken by the opposing side from the place where the offence occurred, unless the offence is committed by a player in his opponents' goal-area, in which case, the free-kick shall be taken from a point anywhere within that half of the goal-area in which the offence occurrred.

Should a player of the defending side intentionally commit one of the above nine offences within the penalty-area he shall be penalized by a **penalty-kick**.

A penalty-kick can be awarded irrespective of the position of the ball, if in play, at the time an offence within the penalty area is committed.

A player committing any of the five following offences:—

1. Playing in a manner considered by the Referee to be dangerous, e.g., attempting to kick the ball while held by the goalkeeper;

2. Charging fairly, i.e., with the shoulder, when the ball is not within playing distance of the players concerned and they are definitely not trying to play it;

3. When not playing the ball, intentionally obstructing an opponent, i.e., running between the opponent and the ball, or interposing the body so as to form an obstacle to an opponent;

4. Charging the goalkeeper except when he:—

   (*a*) is holding the ball;
   (*b*) is obstructing an opponent;
   (*c*) has passed outside his goal-area;

5. When playing as a goalkeeper and within his own penalty-area:

   (*a*) from the moment he takes control of the ball with his hands, he takes more than 4 steps in any direction whilst holding, bouncing or throwing the ball in the air and catching it again, without releasing it into play, or, having released the ball into play before, during or after the 4 steps, he touches it again with his hands, before it has been touched or played by another player of the same team outside of the penalty-area, or by a player of the opposing team either inside or outside of the penalty-area, or

   (*b*) indulges in tactics which, in the opinion of the Referee, are designed merely to hold up the game and thus waste time and so give an unfair advantage to his own team.

shall be penalized by the award of an **indirect free-kick** to be taken by the opposing side from the place where the infringement occurred, subject to the over-riding conditions imposed in Law 13.

On any occasion when a player deliberately kicks the ball to his own goalkeeper, the goalkeeper is not permitted to touch it with his hands. If, however, the goalkeeper does touch the ball with his hands, he shall be penalized by the award of an indirect free kick to be taken by the opposing team from the place where the infringement occurred, subject to the overriding conditions of Law 13.

A player shall be **cautioned** if:—

(*j*) he enters or re-enters the field of play to join or re-join his team after the game has commenced, or leaves the field of play during the progress of the game (except through accident) without, in either case, first having received a signal from the Referee showing him that he may do so. If the Referee stops the game to administer the caution the game shall be restarted by an indirect free-kick taken by a player of the opposing team from the place where the ball was when the Referee stopped the game, subject to the over-riding conditions imposed in Law 13.

If, however, the offending player has committed a more serious offence he shall be penalized according to that section of the law he infringed;

(*k*) he persistently infringes the laws of the Game;

(*l*) he shows by word or action, dissent from any decision given by the Referee;

(*m*) he is guilty of ungentlemanly conduct.

For any of these last three offences, in addition to the caution an **indirect free-kick** shall be awarded to the opposing side from the place where the offence occurred, subject to the over-riding conditions imposed in Law 13, unless a more serious infringement of the Laws of the Game was committed.

A player shall be sent off the field of play if, in the opinion of the Referee, he:—

(*n*) is guilty of violent conduct or serious foul play;

(*o*) uses foul or abusive language;

(*p*) persists in misconduct after having received a caution.

If play be stopped by reason of a player being ordered from the field for an offence without a separate breach of the Law having been committed, the game shall be resumed by an **indirect free-kick** awarded to the opposing side from the place where the infringement occurred, subject to the over-riding conditions imposed in Law 13.

INTERNATIONAL BOARD DECISIONS

1. If the goalkeeper either intentionally strikes an opponent by throwing the ball vigorously at him, or pushes him with the ball while holding it, the Referee shall award a penalty-kick, if the offence took place within the penalty-area.

2. If a player deliberately turns his back to an opponent when he is about to be tackled, he may be charged but not in a dangerous manner.

3. In case of body-contact in the goal area between an attacking player and the opposing goalkeeper not in possession of the ball, the Referee, as sole judge of intention, shall stop the game if, in his opinion, the action of the attacking player was intentional, and award an indirect free-kick.

4. If a player leans on the shoulders of another player of his own team in order to head the ball, the Referee shall stop the game, caution the player for ungentlemanly conduct and award an indirect free-kick to the opposing side.

5. A player's obligation when joining or rejoining his team after the start of the match to 'report to the Referee' must be interpreted as meaning to 'draw the attention of the Referee from the touch-line'. The signal from the Referee shall be made by a definite gesture which makes the player understand that he may come into the field of play; it is not necessary for the Referee to wait until the game is stopped (this does not apply in respect of an infringement of Law 4), but the Referee is the sole judge of the moment in which he gives his signal of acknowledgement.

6. The letter and spirit of Law 12 do not oblige the Referee to stop a game to administer a caution. He may, if he chooses, apply the advantage. If he does apply the advantage, he shall caution the player when play stops.

7. If a player covers up the ball without touching it in an endeavour not to have it played by an opponent, he obstructs but does not infringe Law 12, para. 3, because he is already in possession of the ball and covers it for tactical reasons whilst the ball remains within playing distance. In fact, he is actually playing the ball and does not commit an infringement; in this case, the player may be charged because he is in fact playing the ball.

8. If a player intentionally stretches his arms to obstruct an opponent and

steps from one side to the other, moving his arms up and down to delay his opponent, forcing him to change course, but does not make 'bodily contact' the Referee shall caution the player for ungentlemanly conduct and award an indirect free-kick.

9. If a player intentionally obstructs the opposing goalkeeper, in an attempt to prevent him from putting the ball into play in accordance with Law 12, 5(a), the Referee shall award an indirect free-kick.

10. If after a Referee has awarded a free-kick a player protests violently by using abusive or foul language and is sent off the field, the free kick should not be taken until the player has left the field.

11. Any player, whether he is within or outside the field of play, whose conduct is ungentlemanly or violent, whether or not it is directed towards an opponent, a colleague, the Referee, a Linesman or other person, or who uses foul or abusive language, is guilty of an offence, and shall be dealt with according to the nature of the offence committed.

12. If in the opinion of the Referee a goalkeeper intentionally lies on the ball longer than is necessary, he shall be penalized for ungentlemanly conduct and

(a) be cautioned, and an indirect free-kick awarded to the opposing team;
(b) in case of repetition of the offence, be sent off the field.

13. The offence of spitting at officials or other persons, or similar unseemly behaviour, shall be considered as violent conduct within the meaning of section (n) of Law 12.

14. If, when a Referee is about to caution a player, and before he has done so, the player commits another offence which merits a caution, the player shall be sent off the field of play.

15. If, in the opinion of the Referee, a player who is moving toward his opponents' goal with an obvious opportunity to score a goal is intentionally impeded by an opponent, through unlawful means, i.e. an offence punishable by a free-kick (or a penalty-kick), thus denying the attacking player's team the aforesaid goal-scoring opportunity, the offending player shall be sent off the field of play for serious foul play in accordance with Law 12(n).

16. If, in the opinion of the Referee, a player, other than the goalkeeper within his own penalty-area, denies his opponents a goal, or an obvious goal-scoring opportunity, by intentionally handling the ball, he shall be

sent off the field of play for serious foul play in accordance with Law 12 (*n*).

17. The International F.A. Board is of the opinion that a goalkeeper, in the circumstances described in Law 12, 5(*a*), will be considered to be in control of the ball when he takes possession of the ball by touching it with any part of his hands or arms. Possession of the ball would include the goalkeeper intentionally parrying the ball, but would not include the circumstances where, in the opinion of the Referee, the ball rebounds accidentally from the goalkeeper, for example after he has made a save.

Advice to Referees

A thorough knowledge of this Law is absolutely essential, but its correct application depends on the Referee's ability to make up his mind whether or not a player's action is INTENTIONAL.

Jumping at an opponent and not jumping for the ball is a foul. There is no such thing as accidental jumping at an opponent.

Do not allow players to crowd round you to question your decision or get you to change it.

Although an opponent is entitled to charge the goalkeeper when the latter is in possession of the ball, i.e. holding the ball, it is not permissible for an opponent to kick or to attempt to kick the ball under such circumstances.

Law Thirteen

FREE-KICK

Free-kicks shall be classified under two headings: 'Direct' (from which a goal can be scored direct against the **offending side**), and 'Indirect' (from which a goal cannot be scored unless the ball has been played or touched by a player other than the kicker before passing through the goal).

When a player is taking a direct or an indirect free-kick inside his own penalty-area, all of the opposing players shall be at least ten yards (9.15 m) from the ball and shall remain outside the penalty-area until the ball has been kicked out of the area. The ball shall be in play immediately it has travelled the distance of its own circumference and is beyond the penalty-area. The goalkeeper shall not receive the ball into his hands, in order that he may thereafter kick it into play. If the ball is not kicked direct into play, beyond the penalty-area, the kick shall be retaken.

When a player is taking a direct or an indirect free-kick outside his own penalty-area, all of the opposing players shall be at least ten yards from the ball, until it is in play, unless they are standing on their own goal-line, between the goal-posts. The ball shall be in play when it has travelled the distance of its own circumference.

If a player of the opposing side encroaches into the penalty-area, or within ten yards of the ball, as the case may be, before a free-kick is taken, the Referee shall delay the taking of the kick, until the Law is complied with.

The ball must be stationary when a free-kick is taken, and the kicker shall not play the ball a second time, until it has been touched or played by another player.

Notwithstanding any other reference in these Laws to the point from which a free-kick is to be taken:

1. *Any free-kick awarded to the defending team, within its own goal-area, may be taken from any point within the goal-area.*

2. Any indirect free-kick awarded to the attacking team within its opponent's goal-area shall be taken from the part of the goal-area line which runs parallel to the goal-line, at the point nearest to where the offence was committed.

Punishment

If the kicker, after taking the free-kick, plays the ball a second time before it has been touched or played by another player, an indirect free-kick shall be taken by a player of the opposing team from the spot where the infringement occurred, unless the offence is committed by a player in his opponents' goal-area, in which case, the free-kick shall be taken from *any point within the goal-area.*

INTERNATIONAL BOARD DECISIONS

1. In order to distinguish between a direct and an indirect free-kick, the referee, when he awards an indirect free-kick, shall indicate accordingly by raising an arm above his head. He shall keep his arm in that position until the kick has been taken and retain the signal until the ball has been played or touched by another player or goes out of play.

2. Players who do not retire to the proper distance when a free-kick is

taken must be cautioned and on any repetition be ordered off. It is particularly requested of Referees that attempts to delay the taking of a free-kick by encroaching should be treated as serious misconduct.

3. If, when a free-kick is being taken, any of the players dance about or gesticulate in a way calculated to distract their opponents, it shall be deemed ungentlemanly conduct for which the offender(s) shall be cautioned.

Advice to Referees

A player has been known to kick the ball directly into his own goal from a direct or indirect free-kick, in which case the Referee should award a corner-kick provided that in the case of a free-kick inside the penalty-area the ball had first been kicked into play. Otherwise the free-kick from inside the penalty-area will have to be retaken. If, however, a player kicks the ball directly into his opponents' goal from an indirect free-kick, the Referee should award a goal-kick to the opponents.

Law Fourteen

PENALTY-KICK

A penalty-kick shall be taken from the penalty-mark and, when it is being taken, all players with the exception of the player taking the kick, properly identified, and the opposing goalkeeper, shall be within the field of play but outside the penalty-area, and at least 10 yards from the penalty-mark. The opposing goalkeeper must stand (without moving his feet) on his own goal-line, between the goal-posts, until the ball is kicked. The player taking the kick must kick the ball forward; he shall not play the ball a second time until it has been touched or played by another player. The ball shall be deemed in play directly it is kicked, i.e., when it has travelled the distance of its circumference. A goal may be scored directly from a penalty-kick. When a penalty-kick is being taken during the normal course of play, or when time has been extended at half-time or full-time to allow a penalty-kick to be taken or retaken, a goal shall not be nullified if, before passing between the posts and under the cross-bar, the ball touches either or both of the goal-posts, or the cross-bar, or the goalkeeper, or any combination of these agencies, providing that no other infringement has occurred.

Punishment

For any infringement of this Law:

- (a) by the defending team, the kick shall be retaken if a goal has not resulted;
- (b) by the attacking team, other than by the player taking the kick, if a goal is scored it shall be disallowed and the kick retaken;
- (c) by the player taking the penalty-kick, committed after the ball is in play, a player of the opposing team shall take an indirect free-kick from the spot where the infringement occurred, subject to the over-riding conditions imposed in Law 13.

INTERNATIONAL BOARD DECISIONS

1. When the Referee has awarded a penalty-kick, he shall not signal for it to be taken, until the players have taken up position in accordance with the Law.

2. (a) If, after the kick has been taken, the ball is stopped in its course towards goal, by an outside agent, the kick shall be retaken.

(b) If, after the kick has been taken, the ball rebounds into play, from the goalkeeper, the cross-bar or a goal-post, and is then stopped in its course by an outside agent, the Referee shall stop play and restart it by dropping the ball at the place where it came into contact with the outside agent, unless it was within the goal area at that time, in which case it shall be dropped on that part of the goal area line which runs parallel to the goal-line, at the point nearest to where the ball was when play was stopped.

3. (a) If, after having given the signal for a penalty-kick to be taken, the Referee sees that the goalkeeper is not in his right place on the goal-line, he shall, nevertheless, allow the kick to proceed. It shall be retaken, if a goal is not scored.

(b) If, after the Referee has given the signal for the penalty-kick to be taken, and before the ball has been kicked, the goalkeeper moves his feet, the Referee shall, nevertheless, allow the kick to proceed. It shall be retaken, if a goal is not scored.

(c) If, after the Referee has given the signal for a penalty-kick to be taken, and before the ball is in play, a player of the defending team encroaches into the penalty-area, or within ten yards of the penalty-mark, the Referee shall, nevertheless, allow the kick to proceed. It shall be retaken, if a goal is not scored.

The player concerned shall be cautioned.

4. (a) If, when a penalty-kick is being taken, the player taking the kick is guilty of ungentlemanly conduct, the kick, if already taken, shall be retaken, if a goal is scored.

The player concerned shall be cautioned.

(b) If, after the Referee has given the signal for a penalty-kick to be taken, and before the ball is in play, a colleague of the player taking the kick encroaches into the penalty-area or within ten yards of the penalty-mark, the Referee shall, nevertheless, allow the kick to proceed. If a goal is scored, it shall be disallowed, and the kick retaken.

The player concerned shall be cautioned.

(c) If, in the circumstances described in the foregoing paragraph, the ball rebounds into play from the goalkeeper, the cross-bar or a goal-post, and a goal has not been scored, the Referee shall stop the game, caution the player and award an idirect free-kick to the opposing team from the place where the infringement occurred, subject to the over-riding conditions imposed in Law 13.

5. (a) If, after the Referee has given the signal for a penalty-kick to be taken, and before the ball is in play, the goalkeeper moves from his position on the goal-line, or moves his feet, and a colleague of the kicker encroaches into the penalty-area or within 10 yards of the penalty-mark, the kick, if taken, shall be retaken.

The colleague of the kicker shall be cautioned.

(b) If, after the Referee has given the signal for a penalty-kick to be taken, and before the ball is in play, a player of each team encroaches into the penalty-area, or within 10 yards of the penalty-mark, the kick, if taken, shall be retaken.

The players concerned shall be cautioned.

6. When a match is extended, at half-time or full-time, to allow a penalty-kick to be taken or retaken, the extension shall last until the moment that the penalty-kick has been completed, i.e., until the Referee has decided whether or not a goal is scored, and the game shall terminate immediately the Referee has made his decision.

After the player taking the penalty-kick has put the ball into play, no player other than the defending goalkeeper may play or touch the ball before the kick is completed.

7. When a penalty-kick is being taken in extended time:—

(a) the provisions of all the foregoing paragraphs, except paragraphs 2 (b) and 4 (c) shall apply in the usual way, and

(b) in the circumstances described in paragraphs 2 (b) and 4 (c) the game shall terminate immediately the ball rebounds from the goalkeeper, the cross-bar or the goal-post.

Advice to Referees

This is an important Law; therefore

(a) Remember that if the original offence was sufficiently serious as to justify the player being ordered off the field, the awarding of a penalty-kick does not cancel this measure.

(b) Bear in mind that if the ball hits the goal-post or cross-bar and rebounds into play, the player who took the penalty-kick must not play it again until it has been touched by another player.

Law Fifteen

THROW-IN

When the whole of the ball passes over the touch-line, either on the ground or in the air, it shall be thrown in from the point where it crossed the line, in any direction, by a player of the team opposite to that of the player who last touched it. The thrower at the moment of delivering the ball must face the field of play and part of each foot shall be either on the touch-line or on the ground outside the touch-line. The thrower shall use both hands and shall deliver the ball from behind and over his head. The ball shall be in play immediately it enters the field of play, but the thrower shall not again play the ball until it has been touched or played by another player. A goal shall not be scored direct from a throw-in.

Punishment

(a) If the ball is improperly thrown in the throw-in shall be taken by a player of the opposing team.

(b) If the thrower plays the ball a second time before it has been touched or played by another player, an indirect free-kick shall be taken by a player of the opposing team from the place where the infringement occurred, subject to the over-riding conditions imposed in Law 13.

1. If a player taking a throw-in, plays the ball a second time by handling it within the field of play before it has been touched or played by another player, the Referee shall award a direct free-kick.

2. A player taking a throw-in must face the field of play with some part of his body.

3. If, when a throw-in is being taken, any of the opposing players dance about or gesticulate in a way calculated to distract or impede the thrower, it shall be deemed ungentlemanly conduct, for which the offender(s) shall be cautioned.

4. A throw-in taken from any position other than the point where the ball passed over the touch-line shall be considered to have been improperly thrown in.

Advice to Referees

See that:

The Linesman clearly indicates with his flag by which team the throw-in is to be taken.

Sometimes a ball is thrown by a player directly from a throw-in into his opponents' goal, in which case the Referee should award a goal-kick. If, however, a player throws the ball directly into his own goal, the Referee should award a corner-kick.

Law Sixteen

GOAL-KICK

When the whole of the ball passes over the goal-line excluding that portion between the goal-posts, either in the air or on the ground, having last been played by one of the attacking team, it shall be kicked direct into play beyond the penalty-area from *any point within the goal-area* by a player of the defending team. A goalkeeper shall not receive the ball into his hands from a goal-kick in order that he may thereafter kick it into play. If the ball is not kicked beyond the penalty-area, i.e., direct into play, the kick shall be retaken. The kicker shall not play the ball a second time until it has touched or been played by another player. A goal shall not be scored direct from such a kick. Players of the team opposing that of the player taking the goal-kick shall remain outside the penalty-area until the ball has been kicked out of the penalty-area.

Punishment

If a player taking a goal-kick plays the ball a second time after it has passed beyond the penalty-area, but before it has touched or been played by another player, an indirect free-kick shall be awarded to the opposing team, to be taken from the place where the infringement occurred, subject to the over-riding conditions imposed in Law 13.

INTERNATIONAL BOARD DECISIONS

1. When a goal-kick has been taken and the player who has kicked the ball, touches it again before it has left the penalty-area, the kick has not been taken in accordance with the Law and must be retaken.

Advice to Referees

Show clearly the side from which the kick is to be taken.

Before giving the signal for the kick, make sure that the players and the ball are correctly positioned, i.e., as stated in this Law.

Law Seventeen

CORNER-KICK

When the whole of the ball passes over the goal-line, excluding that portion between the goal-posts, either in the air or on the ground, having last been played by one of the defending team, a member of the attacking team shall take a corner-kick, i.e., the whole of the ball shall be placed within the quarter circle at the nearest corner flag-post, which must not be moved, and it shall be kicked from that position.

A goal may be scored direct from such a kick. Players of the team opposing that of the player taking the corner-kick shall not approach within 10 yards of the ball until it is in play, i.e., it has travelled the distance of its own circumference, nor shall the kicker play the ball a second time until it has been touched or played by another player.

Punishment

(*a*) If the player who takes the kick plays the ball a second time before it has been touched or played by another player, the Referee shall award an indirect free-kick to the opposing team, to be taken from the place where the infringement occurred, subject to the over-riding conditions imposed in Law 13.

(*b*) For any other infringement the kick shall be retaken.

Advice to Referees

Occasionally the ball strikes a goal-post and rebounds to the player who took the kick. The Law states he must not play it again until it has been touched by another player.

If a player, before taking a corner-kick, removes the corner flag-post, order it to be replaced before giving the signal for the corner-kick to be taken.

————

The International Board at its Meeting on 27th June 1970 accepted a proposal by the Federation Internationale de Football Association that the practice of drawing lots to determine which of two teams in a drawn match should proceed to a later stage of a Knock-Out Competition or receive the trophy (if any) be discontinued and be replaced by the taking of kicks from the penalty-mark which shall not be considered part of the match, subject to the following conditions:—

1. The Referee shall choose the goal at which all of the kicks shall be taken.

2. He shall toss a coin, and the team whose captain wins the toss shall take the first kick.

3. The Referee will record the names of the players who have taken the kicks from the penalty mark, in order to ensure that the provisions of article 7, below, are adhered to.

4. (*a*) Subject to the terms of the following paragraphs (*c*) and (*d*) both teams shall take five kicks.

(*b*) The kicks shall be taken alternately.

(*c*) If, before both teams have taken five kicks, one has scored more goals than the other could, even if it were to complete its five kicks, the taking of kicks shall cease.

(*d*) If, after both teams have taken five kicks, both have scored the same number of goals, or have not scored any goals, the taking of kicks shall continue in the same order, until such time as both have taken an equal number of kicks

35

(not necessarily five more kicks) and one has scored a goal more than the other.

5. The team which scores the greater number of goals, whether the number of kicks taken is in accordance with the terms of the foregoing paragraph 4(*a*), 4(*c*) or 4(*d*) shall qualify for the next round of the competition, or shall be declared winner of the competition, as the case may be.

6. (*a*) With the exception referred to in the following paragraph (*b*) only the players who are on the field of play at the end of the match, which shall mean at the end of extra time in so far as a match in which extra time is authorized is concerned, and any who, having left the field temporarily, with or without the referee's permission, are not on the field of play at that time, shall take part in the taking of the kicks.

(*b*) Provided that his team has not already made use of the maximum number of substitutes permitted by the rules of the competition under which the match was played, a goalkeeper who sustains an injury during the taking of the kicks, and who, because of the injury, is unable to continue as goalkeeper may be replaced by a substitute.

7. Each kick shall be taken by a different player, and not until all eligible players of any team, including the goalkeeper or the named substitute by whom he was replaced in terms of paragraph (6) as the case may be, have each taken a kick may a player of the same team take a second kick.

8. Subject to the terms of paragraph (6) any player who is eligible may change places with his goalkeeper at any time during the taking of the kicks.

9. (*a*) Other than the player taking a kick from the penalty mark, and the two goalkeepers, all players shall remain within the centre circle whilst the taking of kicks is in progress.

(*b*) The goalkeeper who is a colleague of the kicker, shall take up position within the field of play, outside the penalty area at which the kicks are being taken, behind the line which runs parallel with the goal-line, and at least 10 yards from the penalty mark.

10. Unless stated to the contrary in the foregong paragraphs 1 to 9, the Laws of the Game, and the International Board Decisions relating thereto, shall, in so far as they can, apply at the taking of the kicks.

N.B. In the event of light failing before the end of the taking of kicks from the penalty mark, the result shall be decided by the toss of a coin or the drawing of lots.

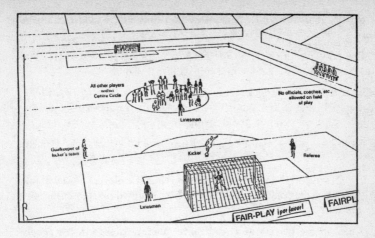

Labels in image: All other players within Centre Circle · Linesman · No officials, coaches, etc., allowed on field of play · Goalkeeper of kicker's team · Kicker · Referee · Linesman · FAIR-PLAY ¡por favor! · FAIRPL

CHECK-LIST FOR REFEREES

1. Decide at which end the kicks will be taken. This can be an important decision if the supporters of one team are behind one goal and those of the other team are at the opposite goal.

2. The team which wins the toss must take the first kick.

3. Before the kicks begin, ensure that all club officials, etc., have left the field and that only the players are left.

4. Make sure all players, apart from the kicker and the two goalkeepers are inside the centre circle.

5. Make sure the goalkeeper of the kicker's team stands outside the penalty area, in the position shown in the diagram.

6. The Laws of the Game, particularly Law 14 'The Penalty-Kick', apply except where modified by the instructions for the taking of kicks from the penalty mark. Be particularly vigilant therefore for instances of gamesmanship or for infringements by the goalkeeper, e.g. moving before the ball is kicked.

7. Keep a careful record of the kicks taken.

8. Where you have the assistance of neutral Linesmen some of those duties may be taken by them, e.g. a Linesman at the centre circle would organize players coming to take the kick while the other Linesman would assist by indicating whether or not the ball has crossed the goal line.

9. It is very important that the referee organizes the taking of kicks from the penalty mark correctly. Make sure you fully understand the instructions.

10. The taking of kicks from the penalty mark never forms part of an actual match. It is only a method of deciding a winner.

11. If, at the taking of kicks from the penalty mark, the light fails badly and the kicks therefore cannot be completed, the result shall be decided by the tossing of a coin or the drawing of lots.

12. An injured player may be excused from the taking of kicks from the penalty mark.

13. It is the responsibility of each team to select the players who will take the kicks from the penalty mark. The Referee's only duty is to ensure that they are taken correctly.

14. When all the players in a team have taken a kick from the penalty mark, it is not necessary that they follow the same order in taking their second kick as they had for the first series of kicks.

15. If a player who has already been cautioned commits a second cautionable offence at the taking of kicks from the penalty mark, he shall be sent off.

16. If the lights fail at a stadium after extra time but before the taking of kicks from the penalty mark, and if they cannot be repaired in a reasonable time, the referee shall decide the match by tossing a coin or drawing lots.

17. A substitute who has not taken part in the match, including extra time where it is played, may not take part in kicks from the penalty mark, except to replace an injured goalkeeper.

18. After each team has taken 10 kicks from the penalty mark, a team which has had a player sent off may use a player who has already taken a kick for the 11th kick.

19. If at the end of the match some players leave the field of play and fail to return for the taking of kicks from the penalty mark, and are not injured, the Referee will not allow the kicks to be taken and will report the matter to the responsible authorities.

20. If, at the taking of kicks from the penalty mark, or when extended time is being allowed for a penalty-kick to be taken in normal playing time, the ball strikes the goal-post or cross-bar, strikes the goalkeeper and enters the goal, a goal shall be awarded.

The signals illustrated in this memorandum have been approved by the International FA Board for use by registered Referees of affiliated National Associations.

Illustrations concerning Signals by the Referee are shown in the illustrated section. They are simple, universally in use, and well understood.

While it is not the duty of the Referee to explain or mime any offence that has caused him to give a particular decision, there are times when a simple gesture or word of guidance can aid communication and assist toward greater understanding, and the gaining of more respect, to the mutual benefit of Referee and players. Improving communication should be encouraged, but the exaggerated miming of offences can be undignified and confusing and should not be used.

An indication by the Referee of the point where a throw-in should be taken may well help prevent a player from taking a throw-in improperly. A call of 'Play on; *advantage*' confirms to a player that the Referee has not missed a foul, but has chosen to apply advantage. Even an indication that the ball was minutely deflected by its touching another player on its path across a touch-line might be helpful too in generating a greater understanding between Referee and players. A better understanding will lead to more harmonious relationships.

All signals given by the Referee should be simple, clear and instinctive. They should be designed to control the game efficiently and to ensure continuous play as far as is possible; they are intended essentially to indicate what the next action in the game should be, not principally to justify that action.

An arm pointing to indicate a corner-kick, goal-kick or foul, and the direction in which it is to be taken, will normally be sufficient. The raised arm to indicate that a free-kick is indirect is clearly understood, but if a player queries politely whether the award is a direct free-kick or an indirect free-kick, a helpful word from the Referee, in addition to the regular signal, will lead to a better understanding in future.

The duties of the Referee and Linesmen are set out briefly but clearly in the Laws of the Game, Laws 5 and 6.

There is further exposition of co-operation between the Referee and Linesmen in the memorandum explaining the universally adopted system of 'diagonal control'.

The proper use of the whistle, voice and hand signals by the Referee and the flags by the Linesmen should all assist understanding through clear communication.

Co-operation between Linesmen and Referee

When play has been stopped the Linesman should assist the Referee by signalling in the following manner for the following incidents:

1. Off-side. The Linesman should lower his flag at full arm's length to the positions illustrated, and point across the field of play to indicate the spot from which the kick should be taken. The only exception would be where the Referee has decided to position himself to judge off-side when play develops from a corner-kick, penalty-kick or free-kick close to goal.

2. Throw-in. When the ball goes out of play over the touch-line on his side of the field, the Linesman should indicate the direction of the throw. He should also signal if the thrower's feet, at the moment of release of the ball, are incorrectly placed.

3. Corner and goal-kicks. When the whole of the ball goes out of play over the goal-line the Linesman should indicate whether a corner-kick or goal-kick should be given.

4. Goal. When the Referee indicates that a goal is scored the Linesman should return quickly to his position towards the half-way line.
Law 12. If the Linesman senses that the Referee has not seen an infringement he should raise his flag high. If the Referee stops play the Linesman shall incidate the direction of the free-kick (direct, or indirect), otherwise he shall lower his flag.

5. Substitution. When a substitution is to be made the Linesman nearest to the point of substitution shall attract the attention of the Referee by raising his flag as shown in the illustration included in 'Signals by the Linesmen'.

The Role of the Fourth Official

1. He would be appointed under the rules of a competition and would officiate in the event of any of the three match officials being unable to continue.

2. The organizer, prior to the start of the competition, should state clearly whether, in the event of any Referee being unable to continue, the fourth official would take over as the match Referee or whether the senior Linesman would take over as Referee with the fourth official becoming a Linesman.

3. The fourth official would assist with any administrative duties before, during and after the match as required by the Referee.

4. He would be responsible for assisting with substitution procedures during the match.

5. He would control the replacement footballs where required. If during a match the match ball had to be replaced he would, on the instructions of the Referee, provide another ball thus keeping the time delay to a minimum.

6. He would have the authority to check the equipment of substitutes prior to them entering the field of play. In the event of their equipment not being within the Laws of the Game he would inform the Linesman who would then inform the Referee.

7. While the fourth official has no status within the Laws of the Game, his duties should be to assist the Referee at all times.

Co-operation between Referee and Linesmen – Law 6

In the Laws of the Game set out in the foregoing pages there are no instructions as to the relative positioning of Referee and Linesmen during a game. There are, however, instructions in Laws 5 and 6 with regard to powers and duties of Referees and Linesmen which rightly interpreted would mean co-operation. Law 6 stipulates that two Linesmen shall be appointed, whose duty (subject to the decision of the Referee) shall be:

(a) To indicate WHEN the ball is out of play.

(b) To indicate when the ball has crossed the goal-line and whether a corner-kick or a goal-kick is to be awarded.

(c) To indicate which side is entitled to the throw-in.

(d) To assist the Referee in carrying out the game in accordance with the Laws.

The assistance referred to in (d) is:

(1) Signalling when the WHOLE of the ball is out of play.

(2) Indicating WHICH side is entitled to the corner-kick, the goal-kick, or the throw-in.

(3) Calling the attention of the Referee to rough play or ungentlemanly conduct.

(4) Giving an opinion on any point on which the Referee may consult him.

(5) **Substitution.** When a substitution is to be made, the Linesman nearest to the point of substitution shall attract the attention of the Referee by raising his flag as shown in the illustration included in 'Signals by the Linesmen'.

Neutral Linesmen

The assistance referred to above is best given by NEUTRAL LINESMEN. A limitation is placed upon CLUB LINESMEN because points (2), (3) and (4) are not usually referred to Linesmen who are not neutral. In the case of Neutral Linesmen they must be used as ASSISTANT REFEREES. It is appreciated that there must be a different attitude adopted by the Referee in this case, because in effect there are THREE officials supervising the play; the REFEREE remains as principal official, but the Linesmen are there to assist him to control the game in a proper manner.

Club Linesmen

To get the most effective co-operation from CLUB LINESMEN the following procedure should be adopted:

(1) BOTH Club Linesmen should report to the Referee BEFORE the start of the match, and receive his instructions, and be informed that no matter what

may be their personal opinion the decision of the Referee is final, and must not be questioned.

(2) The work allotted to them as Club Linesmen is to signal WHEN the ball is ENTIRELY over the touch-line, and to indicate WHICH side is entitled to the throw-in, subject always to the decisions of the Referee.

Keeping in mind their distinctive duties outlined above Referees should decide beforehand exactly WHAT they want their Club Linesmen to do, and should be able to tell them distinctly how they can best help him. It is essential that there should be some conference between the three officials BEFORE any match. As the chief of this trio, the Referee must be able to indicate clearly to his assistants how they may best help him. His instructions must be specific, in order to avoid confusion. On their side, the LINESMEN must fully appreciate the Referee's prior authority, and accept his rulings without question, should there be any difference of opinion amongst them. Their relationship to him MUST be one of assistance and neither undue intervention nor opposition.

The Referee will operate the diagonal system of control when his Linesmen are neutral. When they are not neutral he shall inform them which method he intends to operate. He will co-operate with his Linesmen on the following matters and indicate to them:–

(a) The time by his watch.

(b) The side of the field which each Linesman will take in each half of the match.

(c) Their duties prior to the commencement of the game, such as the examination of the appurtenances of the game.

(d) Which shall be the senior Linesman in case of need.

(e) The position to be taken for corner-kicks.

(f) The sign that he has noticed his Linesman, but has overruled the indication therefrom.

(g) Which action in the throw-in shall be in the province of the Linesman, and which that of the Referee, e.g., many Referees ask their Linesmen to watch for foot-faults whilst they look for the hand-faults.

Referees should not necessarily keep to one diagonal of the field of play. If the state of the ground, wind, sun or other conditions demand a change to the opposite diagonal, a Referee should indicate to his Linesmen his intention to make such a change-over, and the Linesmen will at once take over the other half of their particular lines. One advantage of such a change of diagonal is that the surface of the ground, next to the touch-line, will be less severely worn because the whole length of the field will be utilized.

Other co-operative matters may be added, but it is important that each of these should be known to the three officials.

The following diagrams illustrate the diagonal system of control, and if studied and practised will lead to uniform methods of control.

Diagram One

The imaginary diagonal used by the Referee is the line A–B.

The opposite diagonal used by the Linesman is adjusted to the position of the Referee; if the Referee is near A, Linesman L2 will be at a point between M and K. When the Referee is at B, Linesman L1 will be between E and F; this gives TWO officials control of the respective 'danger zones', one at each side of the field.

Linesman L1 adopts the REDS as his side; Linesman L2 adopts the BLUES; as RED forwards move towards BLUE goal, Linesman L1 keeps up with their foremost man, so in actual practice he will rarely get into RED's half of the field. Similarly Linesman L2 keeps up with the foremost BLUE player, and will rarely get into BLUE's half.

At corner-kicks or penalty-kicks the Linesman in that half where the corner-kick or penalty-kick occurs positions himself at N and the Referee takes position (see Diagram 4 – corner-kick; Diagram 9 – penalty-kick).

The diagonal system fails if Linesman L2 gets between G and H when Referee is at B, or when Linesman L1 is near C or D when the Referee is at A, because there are TWO officials at the same place. This should be avoided.

(N.B. – Some Referees prefer to use the opposite diagonal, viz., from F to M, in which case the Linesmen should adjust their work accordingly.)

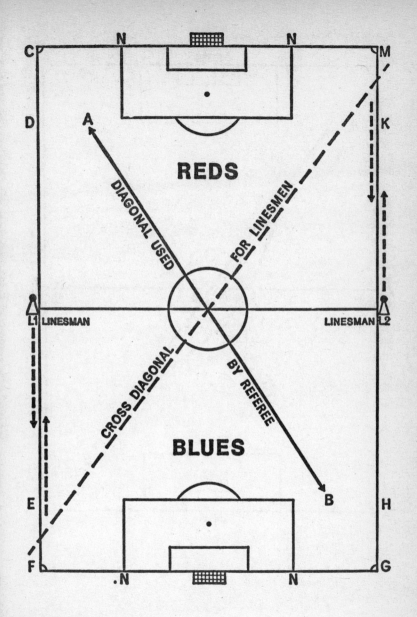

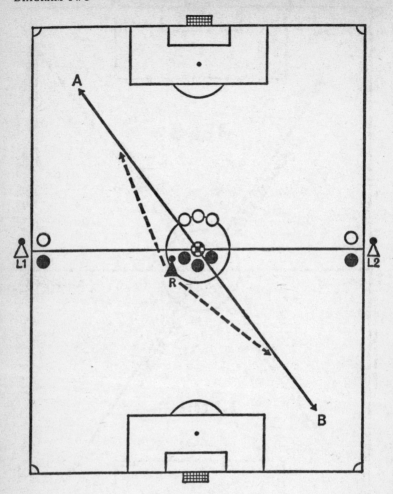

START OF GAME

Position of Referee at Kick-off – R.
Position of Linesmen – L1 and L2.
Players – ○ and ●.
Diagonal followed by Referee – A —— B.
Referee moves to diagonal along line ←— —→ according to direction of attack.
Ball – ⊛.

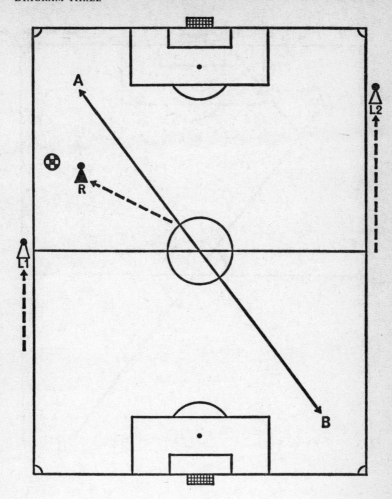

DEVELOPMENT OF ATTACK

(From Diagram 2)

Ball moves out to left wing, Referee (R) slightly off diagonal to be near play.
Linesman (L2) level with spearhead of attack.
Two officials, therefore, up with play.
Linesman (L1) in position for clearance and possible counter attack.

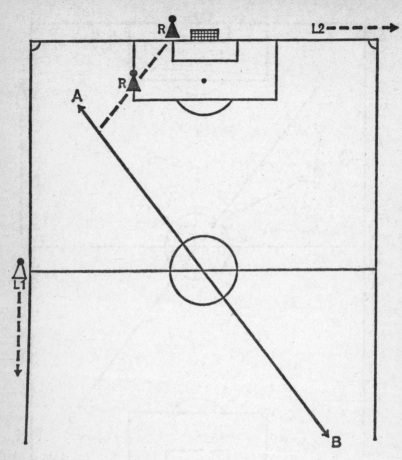

CORNER-KICK

Position of officials the same no matter at which corner-area the kick is taken. Referee (R) alongside goal-post, or at position shown.

Concerning the position of the Linesman No. 2, in accordance with the instructions from the Referee the Linesman No. 2 (L2) shall be near the corner flag or on the goal-line near the corner flag, to observe whether the ball is properly played, whether the opposing players are at proper distance (10 yards), whether the ball is behind the goal-line, or whether incidents have happened possibly hidden from the Referee.

Linesman (L1) in position for clearance and possible counter attack.

Play On − Advantage. Where the referee sees an offence but uses the Advantage, he shall indicate that play shall continue

Indirect Free-kick. This signal shall be maintained until the kick has been taken and retained until the ball has been played or touched by another player or goes out of play

Direct Free-kick. The hand and arm clearly indicate the direction

Penalty-kick. The referee clearly indicates the penalty-mark, but there is no need to run towards it

Goal-kick

Corner-kick

Caution or Expulsion. With the card system in operation, the card shall be shown in the manner illustrated. The player's identity *must* be recorded at the time

Off-side. Flag held upright to indicate Off-side

Off-side. When the referee stops play, linesman indicates position on far side of the field

Off-side. Position on near side of the field

Off-side. Position near the centre of the field

Throw-in

Back view of the linesman signalling to the referee for a substitution to be made

Front view of the linesman signalling to the referee when a substitute is waiting at the lines

Goal-kick

Corner-kick. The linesman may first need to signal that the ball has gone out of play if there is any doubt. He should also look at the referee in case he has already made his own decision which may be different from the linesman's

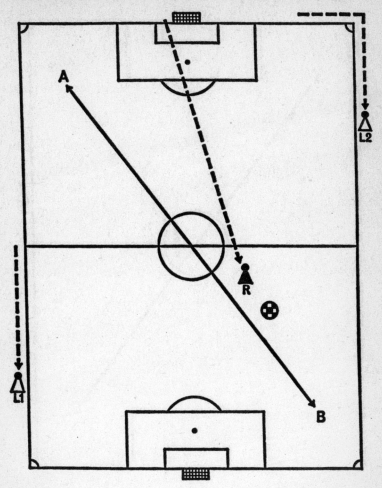

THE COUNTER-ATTACK

(Following Diagram 4)

Referee (R) sprints to regain correct position on diagonal along path — — —→ (Note: The Referee who is physically fit is able to do this easily.)

Linesman (L2) hurries back to his correct position on the touch-line.

Linesman (L1) level with attack and in position to see infringements and indicate decisions until Referee regains his position.

DIAGRAM SIX

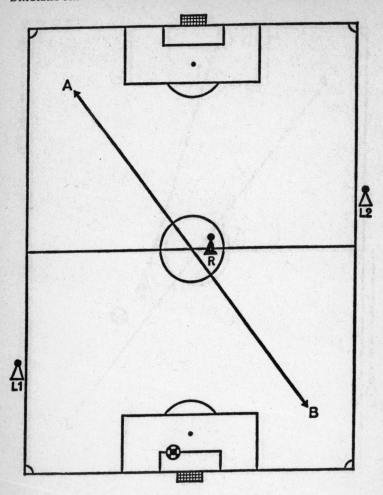

GOAL-KICK

Referee (R) in midfield adjacent to central point of diagonal.
Linesman (L1) exercising watch over goal-kick.
Linesman (L2) in position pending a possible attack by side taking goal-kick.

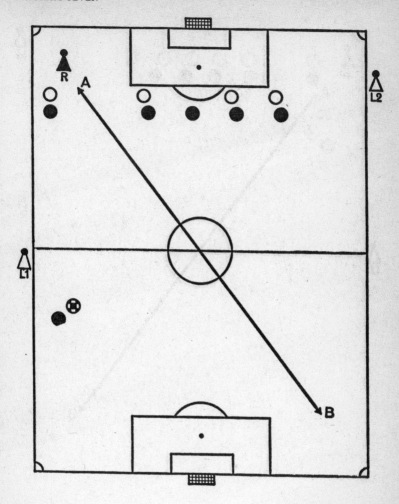

FREE-KICK IN MIDFIELD

Players lined up for kick ● and ○. Referee (R) and Linesman (L2) in respective diagonal positions, level with players and able to judge accurately any questions of off-side or foul play. Linesman (L1) sees that kick is taken from correct position and also is in position for possible counter attack.

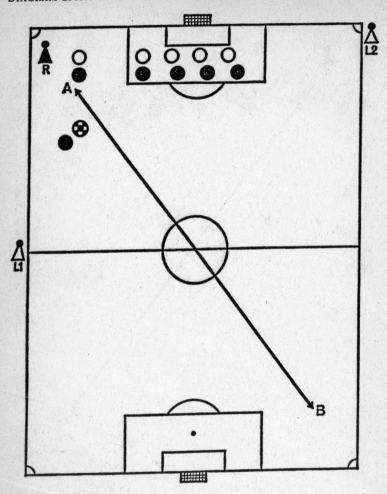

FREE-KICK NEAR GOAL

(Just outside penalty-area)

Players ● and ○ line up for free-kick.

Referee (R) takes up his position just off his diagonal so that he is placed accurately to judge off-side. Linesman (L2) is more advanced but can watch for off-side and fouls and also is in a good position to act as goal judge in the event of a direct shot being taken.

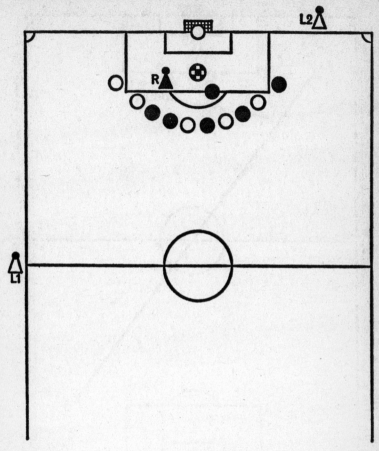

PENALTY-KICK

Players ● and ○ with the exception of the goalkeeper and kicker are shown outside the penalty area and at least 10 yards from the ball – goalkeeper on goal-line.

Referee (R) is in position to see that kick is properly taken and that no encroachment takes place.

Linesman (L2) watches goalkeeper to see that he does not advance illegally and also acts as goal judge.

Linesman (L1) is in position should the goalkeeper save a goal and start a counter attack.

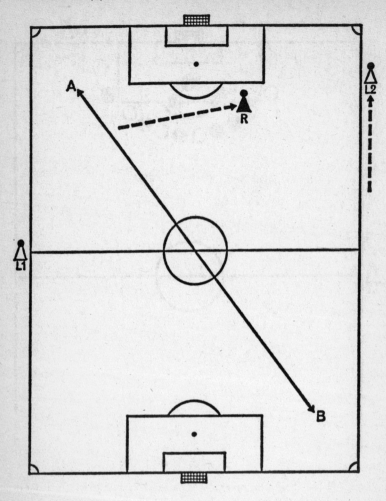

THROW-IN

Ball out of play and Linesman (L2) is in position to indicate position of throw and to which side.

Referee (R) crosses from diagonal to centre of field, in the same manner as a defence covering a throw-in.

Linesman (L1) watches his forward line against the possible counter attack.

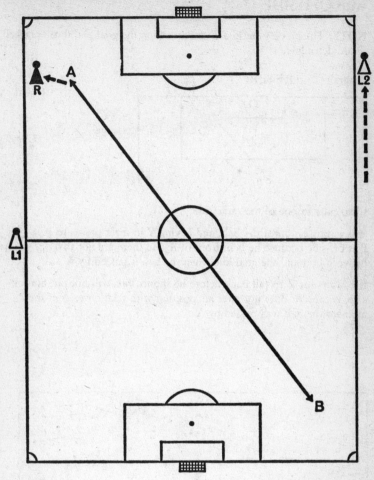

THROW-IN

Linesman (L1) is away from the throw-in but should be able to judge feet and probably to indicate which side is entitled to throw. He also maintains his position in the event of a clearance.

Referee (R) can judge other throw-in infringements and veers slightly from his diagonal towards touch-line.

Linesman (L2) is in position to see any infringement occurring before Referee can turn to follow play.

Diagrams illustrating points in connection with OFF-SIDE

NOTE: The players marked ⊗ are attacking the goal and those marked ○ are defending.

Diagram 1 – OFF-SIDE

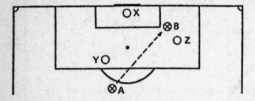

Clear pass to one of the same side

A is in possession of the ball, and having **Y** in front passes to **B**.
B is off-side because he is in front of **A** and there are not two opponents between him and the goal-line when the ball is passed by **A**.

If **B** waits for **Z** to fall back before he shoots, this will not put him on-side, because it does not alter his position with relation to **A** at the moment the ball was passed by **A**.

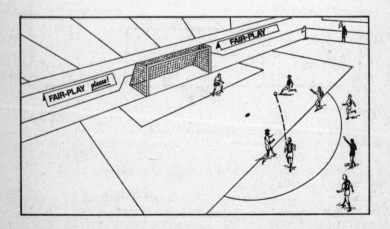

Diagram 2 – NOT OFF-SIDE

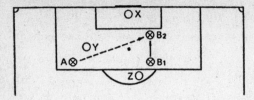

Clear pass to one of the same side (continued)

A is in possession of the ball, and having Y in front passes across the field. B runs from position 1 to position 2.

B is not off-side because at the moment the ball was passed by A he was not in front of the ball, and had two opponents between him and the goal-line.

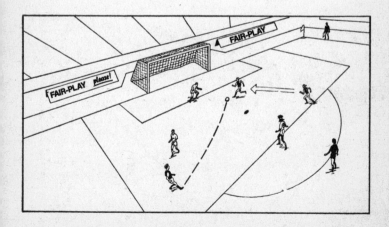

Diagram 3 – OFF-SIDE

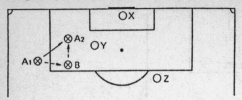

Clear pass to one of the same side (continued)

A and B make a passing run up the wing. A passes the ball to B who cannot shoot because he has **Y** in front. A then runs from position 1 to position 2 and B then passes the ball to him.

A is off-side because he is in front of the ball and there are not two opponents between him and the goal-line when the ball was played by **B**.

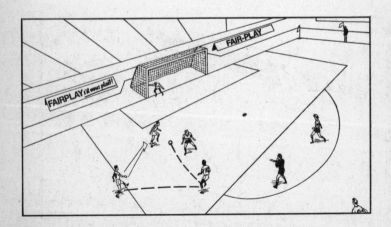

Diagram 4 – NOT OFF-SIDE

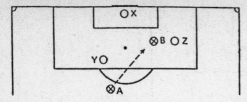

Clear pass to one of the same side (continued)

A is in possession of the ball, and having Y in front passes to B.

B is not off-side because he is not nearer to his opponents' goal-line than at least two opponents when the ball is passed by A.

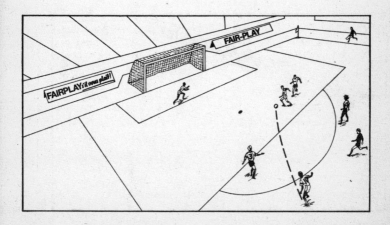

Diagram 5 – NOT OFF-SIDE

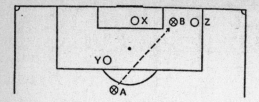

Clear pass to one of the same side (continued)

A is in possession of the ball, and having **Y** in front passes to **B**.

B is not off-side because he is level with **X** and **Z** when the ball is passed by **A** and is therefore not nearer his opponents' goal-line than at least two of his opponents.

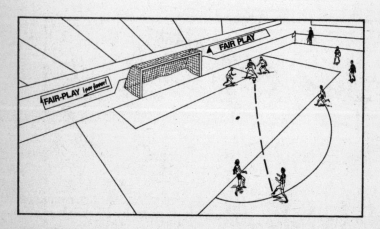

Diagram 6 – OFF-SIDE

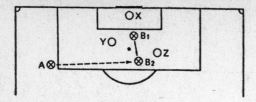

Running back for the ball

A centres the ball. B runs back from position 1 to position 2, and then dribbles between Y and Z and scores.

B is off-side because he is in front of the ball and there were not two opponents between him and the goal-line at the moment the ball was played by A.

Diagram 7 – OFF-SIDE

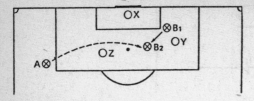

Running back for the ball (continued)

A makes a high shot at goal, and the wind and screw carry the ball back. B runs from position 1 to position 2 and scores.

B is off-side because he is front of the ball and there were not two opponents between him and the goal-line at the moment the ball was played by A.

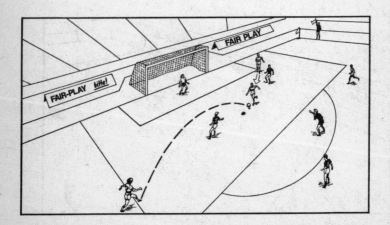

Diagram 8 – OFF-SIDE

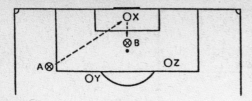

Shot at goal returned by goalkeeper (X)

A shoots at goal. The ball is played by X and B obtains possession.

B is off-side because he was in front of A when the ball was played by A and B did not have two opponents between him and the goal-line.

Diagram 9 – OFF-SIDE

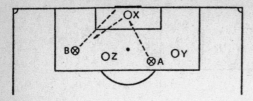

Shot at goal returned by goalkeeper (continued)

A shoots at goal. The ball is played out by X but B obtains possession and scores.

The goal should be disallowed if the referee considers that B, who is in an off-side position when A shoots, is interfering with play.

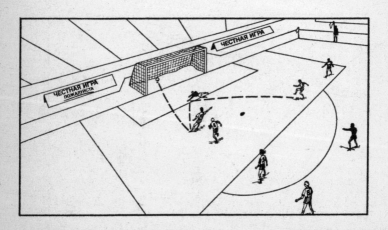

Diagram 10 – OFF-SIDE

Ball rebounding from goal-posts or cross-bar

A shoots for goal and the ball rebounds from the goal-post into play.
B secures the ball and scores.

B is off-side because the ball is last played by A, a player of his own side, and when A played it B was in front of the ball and did not have two opponents between him and the goal-line.

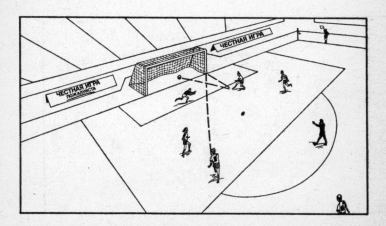

Diagram 11 – OFF-SIDE

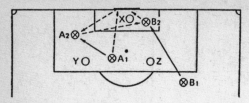

Ball rebounding from goal-posts or cross-bar (continued)

A shoots for goal and the ball rebounds from the cross-bar into play. A follows up from position 1 to position 2, and then passes to B who has run up on the other side.

B is off-side because the ball is last played by A, a player of his own side, and when A played it B was in front of the ball and did not have two opponents between him and the goal-line. If A kicks the ball directly into the goal from his new position instead of passing to B the Referee should award a goal if he considers that B in his new position at B2 is neither interfering with play or an opponent nor seeking to gain an advantage.

Diagram 12 — OFF-SIDE

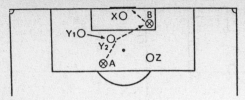

Ball touching an opponent

A shoots at goal. Y runs from position 1 to position 2 to intercept the ball, but it glances off his foot to B who scores.

B is off-side as he was in an off-side position at the moment the ball was played by one of his own team and interfering with play notwithstanding that the ball was deflected by Y.

Diagram 13 – OFF-SIDE

Obstructing the goalkeeper

A shoots for goal and scores. **B**, however, obstructs **X** so that he cannot get at the ball.

The goal must be disallowed, because **B** is in an off-side position and may not touch the ball himself, nor in any way whatever interfere with an opponent.

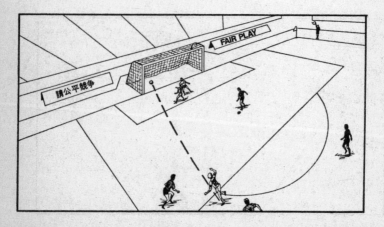

Diagram 14 – OFF-SIDE

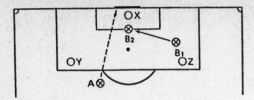

Obstructing the goalkeeper (continued)

A shoots for goal. B runs in while the ball is in transit and prevents X playing it properly.

B is off-side because he is in front of A and there are not two opponents between him and the goal-line when A plays the ball. When in this position B may not touch the ball himself, nor in any way whatever interfere with an opponent.

Diagram 15 – OFF-SIDE

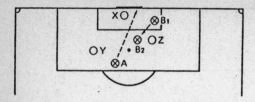

Obstructing an opponent other than the goalkeeper

A shoots for goal. B prevents Z running in to intercept the ball.

B is off-side because he is in front of A and there are not two opponents between him and the goal-line when A plays the ball. When in this position, B may not touch the ball himself nor in any way whatever interfere with an opponent.

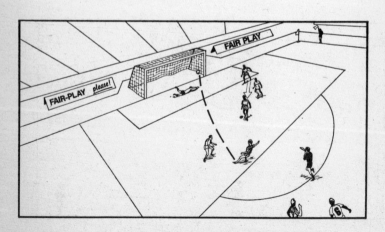

Diagram 16 – OFF-SIDE

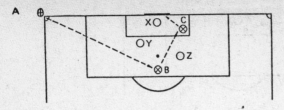

After a corner-kick

A takes a corner-kick and the ball goes to **B**. **B** shoots for goal and as the ball is passing through, **C** touches it.

C is off-side because after the corner-kick has been taken the ball is last played by **B**, a player of his own side, and when **B** played it **C** was in front of the ball and there were not two opponents between him and the goal-line.

Diagram 17 – NOT OFF-SIDE

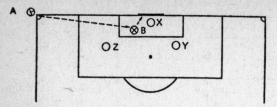

After a corner-kick (continued)

A takes a corner-kick and the ball goes to **B**, who scores.

B has only one opponent between him and the goal-line, but he is not off-side because a player cannot be off-side from a corner-kick.

Diagram 18 – NOT OFF-SIDE

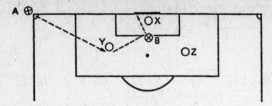

After a corner-kick (continued)

A takes a corner-kick and the ball glances off Y and goes to B, who scores.

The goal should be allowed as B was not off-side when the ball was last played by a member of his own team.

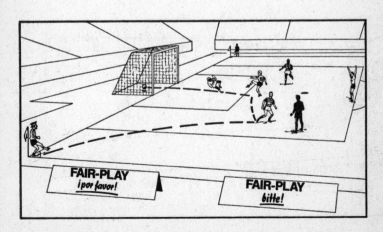

Diagram 19 – OFF-SIDE

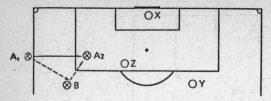

After a throw-in from the touch-line

A throws to B and then runs from the touch-line to position **A2**.
B passes the ball to A in position **2**.

A is off-side because he is in front of the ball and there are not two opponents between him and the goal-line when the ball is passed forward to him by B.

Diagram 20 – NOT OFF-SIDE

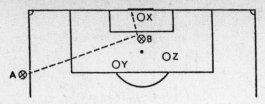

After a throw-in from the touch-line (continued)

A throws the ball to **B**.

Although **B** is in front of the ball and there are not two opponents between him and the goal-line, he is not off-side because a player cannot be off-side from a throw-in.

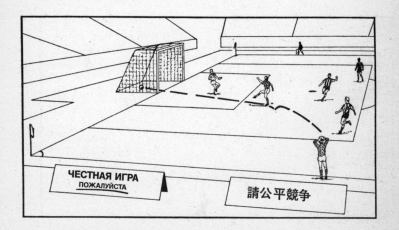

Diagram 21 – OFF-SIDE

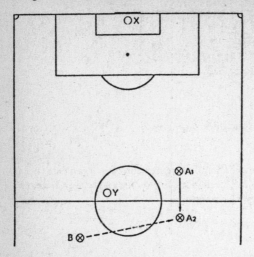

A player cannot put himself on-side by running back into his own half of the field of play.

If **A** is in his opponents' half of the field of play and is off-side in that position when **B** last played the ball, he cannot put himself on-side by moving back into his own half of the field of play.

Diagram 22 – NOT OFF-SIDE

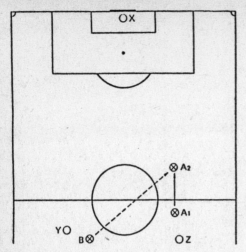

A player within his own half of the field of play is not off-side when he enters his opponents' half of the field of play.

If **A** is in his own half of the field of play he is on-side, although he is in front of the ball and there are not two opponents nearer their own goal-line when **B** last played the ball. **A** is therefore not off-side when he enters his opponents' half of the field of play.